Table of Contents

Preface

Why should you read this book?

Its a fair question and the answer is straight forward: I believe that our future depends on it!

All of our lives depend on these concepts being talked about and built upon. Humanity will not survive unless we change the fundamental way in which we live.

It makes sense to educate yourself with a perspective on world peace if you are truly interested in having world peace. If you were really interested in learning to sail, then you may read a book on how to sail or take lessons. If your were interested in learning how to heal, you would likely read books on that subject. Similarly, if you really want to learn how to live a better life and achieve world peace, it stands to reason that you will read about perspectives on world peace.

After spending a great deal of time researching, thinking and observing, I have come to the conclusion that most of the issues that stand in the way of world peace are related to the monetary consumerism paradigm in which we live.

If you and I met and we each had 1 dollar. And we exchanged that dollar, we would each still have 1 dollar. If we each had 1 idea and shared that idea, we would each have 2 ideas. This is why we must design our lives socially and functionally on intellectual value not monetary value. If you met with a group of say 10 people and you each had 10 ideas to share, you would leave with 100 ideas and so would each of the people in the group! Those 100 ideas would perhaps inspire each of the 10 people with many more ideas and the process continues. The intellectual exchange is exponentially advantageous!

No amount of money can feed you when you are hungry, quench your thirst or keep you from drowning in the sea when you have no way to stay afloat. Many wealthy people have perished because they did not have the one idea or the cooperation of another that could save them.

This book is designed to help us to wake up and see the absurdity of the life that we are living and to realize that we can choose to live this life very differently. We are all subjects of modern day slavery and humanity is at a cross road.

We can either choose to continue being asleep and mindlessly play the game that we were born into or we can choose to play a whole new game! World peace can only be achieved if we choose to live life by a whole new design.

Einstein defined insanity as: "Doing the same things over and over again expecting different results". As long as we play the game the same way then we are part of that insanity.

I hope that this short read will help you to understand that we have very little time left to avoid catastrophic disaster on a global scale and also that world peace is truly attainable.

Let's design a life for our children and grandchildren that ensures that they thrive!

It is very important to me that you do not see this book as another pessimistic look at the world spreading gloom and doom.

In every crisis the opportunity for something good to be created emerges. In the crisis that our world is presently facing, we have the incredible opportunity to evolve our way of living to have a great life experience!

I invite you to create that great life experience for yourself and all the generations to follow.

Join me in the quest, visit: http://thenewgame.org and become part of the solution!

Also: search for **"the new game"** on Facebook.

Thank you friends and family for your patience, understanding and for your help in making this book and this movement a reality!

My wife Robin – For being my best friend and for kindly tolerating my obsessive behavior. Also for your true love and keeping me grounded!

Ron Bianchi, Yvette Ellsworth, Jennifer Betts, Rhonda Coulier, Michael Ross

Chapter 1 –Surviving

At the time that I began writing this book (March, 2011), I was contemplating the many dooms-day scenarios that were gaining popularity in the world. I have also read about many people who believe that the next few years are important for humanity in an evolutionary or spiritual sense.

I started to wonder to myself if humanity was suddenly becoming self aware. Because of technology and our newly found ability to communicate and exchange information at such accelerated speed, maybe our species is ready to consciously evolve!

At the same time, I am watching the insanity all around me in rural Michigan and seeing horrific behaviors of people around the world. I'm seeing the tsunami in Japan kill thousands and I wonder how much this catastrophic event lends itself to the dooms-day predictions that are gaining such popularity.

Without question, many of us feel like something BIG is about to happen. When you combine the social economic unrest and severe climatic changes of the Earth with the fear of many who believe that the end of the Mayan calendar signifies the end of the world, you certainly could get caught up in it all!

Many people are seriously concerned about what may happen on December 21st, 2012. Above all the hype and speculation there are murmurings of science and collective reasoning that stand out if only in their observation.

Humanity has predicted the end of the world nearly since the beginning and many dooms-day events have come and gone leaving nothing in their wake except the wonder of it all. Our obsession with the end makes me wonder sometimes if we are in so much pain living our daily lives that we all but hope the end is near so that there is a conclusion.

If you haven't been following the news and speculation, here is a brief synopsis as I understand it: The Mayan calendar is said to be the most sophisticated calendar ever created by any known civilization. It is more accurate than the modern calendar that we use today. The Mayans were obsessed with time and astrology and they were amazingly accurate with their documentation and prediction of some astrological events. Today, science is fascinated by this ancient culture's ability.

Some believe that on December 21st, 2012 the Mayans predicted that certain planets will align with the Earth in such a way as to cause flooding on a global scale. Others believe that the Mayans predicted that this is just a great cycle of change. Still others believe that the end of the Mayan calendar signifies the absolute end of civilization.

According to the scientific community, there is an event that happens about every 26,000 years where the Earth will complete its "wobble" on its axis. The cycle of this wobble is known as "precession." Scientists say that this could be the cycle of change that the Mayans predicted.

Okay, so now, the big question; What does it all mean? Well, strictly based on what we know, not much. Many of the interpretations of the Mayan calendar signifying the end of the world and all the hype is just that, "Hype"! I personally believe that December 21st, 2012 in most respects will be just another day. It's no more likely that there will be some incredible cataclysmic event that will change the world in a flash than at any other time. Well, unless mass hysteria rules the day or terrorists decide that is the day they want to fulfill their prophecies and exploit the opportunity.

We live in a world that is very volatile and there is a great deal of human suffering going on that could lead to a cataclysmic event. We also know that extreme climate changes are capable of creating a cataclysmic event. Global financial markets are collapsing and money is being created out of thin air leaving bad debt and inflation in its wake. Social unrest is also at an all time high around the globe! Will any one or all of these things cause the world as we know it to end in 2012?

It's anyone's guess! What is certain is the course we are on with global social economic unrest along with a planet that is under great climatic stress means we are headed for some real challenges.

I believe that the timing of all the 2012 hype certainly could mark one of mankind's great moments in time but in a very different way. I believe that this is an opportunity for all of humanity to reflect on what we are, where we have been and for the first time ever, to formulate a better plan for the collective good of all humanity. I believe that this is a golden opportunity for humanity to transition into a state of being that will ensure the very survival of our species!

What if we knew without a doubt that the world would end on a specific date? I think if it were absolute and everyone knew, then we would all start living life very differently. I believe that wars would stop instantly. People would behave more kindly to each other. Most everyone would spend more time and effort with their loved ones. And for awhile, life would be better than it has ever been! Of course, there would still be those who would riot, kill, rape and pillage. I personally do not understand that type of "animal mentality" but that doesn't mean that it doesn't exist. I'm fairly certain that people of that mentality are not reading this book, or any book for that matter. And, whatever anyone has to say would not impact their behaviors whatsoever.

I believe that most people would value every minute of every day. The things that we once thought important would no longer have meaning and the only thing that would really matter is our relationships and how good we could live each day.

We wouldn't be concerned with how much money we could make in our last few days on Earth. We wouldn't be concerned about paying the electric bill or who owed us money.

We wouldn't call the police about the guy next door smoking pot or complain about the neighbor not mowing his lawn.

We may take a little more time to thank the person that makes our day a little better by selflessly serving us.

We may even choose to serve someone else to make their day brighter.

If we had a significant amount of time, say 2 years before the world ended. But we knew with absolute certainty that it would in fact end at that date. I wonder how we may adjust our social behaviors and how we may redefine our values?

I believe that we may stop thinking in terms of profit and start thinking in terms of cooperation and working toward common goals for all humanity!

No matter the cost, I believe that all of humanity would work to ensure the survival of our species.

Would money even matter to anyone anymore?

Would we care to compete with each other to see who is the smartest, strongest or most beautiful?

Would we care about which famous person slept with another?

Would we care who believes in worshiping cows versus who worships Christ?

Would we care at all about how much it was going to cost to somehow avoid the end of humanity on that last day?

Do you think that anything at all would get in the way of our working together to figure out how to ensure the survival of humanity?

In the end, money won't buy you an opportunity to survive. The only chance you have to survive is through cooperation and a contribution to the common goal of survival.

I wonder... why do we think that we have to wait for an imminent end date before we start living life peacefully and cooperatively?

Chapter 2 –Imagine World Peace

One day before doing what I call: "getting on the hamster wheel," I pondered for a couple of hours the idea that I am a slave! It was a grim thought. I was quite devastated and I was almost paralyzed with distress. I had not thought of myself this way.

It struck me that I was just like nearly everyone else in the world who must work for money in order to live. My life boils down to being a slave so that I can make more money and consume more stuff!

I trade the one thing that I have more of right now than I ever will again, for something that will be short-lived at best. I'm talking about "time" of course.

Our time on Earth is the one thing we have more of right now than we ever will again. Most of our time is not even remembered because we are on auto-pilot. We wake up, go to work, come home, eat, maybe have a couple of hours of entertainment, then sleep and we do it all over again. We may occasionally have a significant moment but generally, most every day looks like the day before. I spend more time doing my job than I spend with my family and friends.

We only remember the moments of good and bad that stand out in our lives. I'm willing to bet that many are like me and can't even remember more than a dozen or so moments throughout the past year! After a couple of hours of pondering, I went into work and fell right back into the routine.

So... what does this have to do with world peace? It has everything to do with it!

As long as we continue to live the paradigms that we currently live, we will not have a chance of achieving world peace. We will continue to live out our lives as slaves to the paradigms. However, we are only held to these current paradigms if we fail to recognize them or if we continue to choose to be part of them.

par·a·digm
n.
1. One that serves as a pattern or model.
2. A set or list of all the inflectional forms of a word or of one of its grammatical categories: the paradigm of an irregular verb.
3. A set of assumptions, concepts, values, and practices that constitutes a way of viewing reality for the community that shares them, especially in an intellectual discipline.
(thefreedictionary.com)

Now, more than ever before, we have the opportunity to shift the paradigms that enslave us and bring about world peace.

Everyone says that they want world peace. Really, if you ask anyone the question: "Would you like to see world peace?," they will all give you the same answer. The answer is always "yes" and it is usually accompanied by the sad resolve that they do not believe it is possible.

Here is something to contemplate with regard to why it is essential to imagine world peace if you really want to have it:

We are spinning through space on this little blue ball a million times smaller than the closest star that gives us life.

We are one of billions of people on Earth. Our Earth is just one planet in a solar system which is one of billions of solar systems in our Milkyway Galaxy each with stars and planets of their own.

And our Milkyway Galaxy is just one of billions of galaxies throughout the universe.

We are literally one of billions and billions and billions.

This realization may make you feel pretty small! Yet, the only thing that makes us small is that we can be small minded.

Each of our brains has as many neural connections as there are stars in our galaxy. Yet we cannot seem to imagine the possibility for a world that is peaceful and cooperative.

Mankind lived in caves until we imagined into reality that we could build homes and eventually, magnificent structures. Even today we look at the ancient pyramids and cities with awe and wonder.

We imagined roads and great cities with shining buildings that touch the sky and now they are common place.

We imagined ourselves traveling to and landing on the moon when we could barely build the computers and technology necessary to support our vision.

There is a reliable and proven system of imagining what we want into reality.

We imagine ourselves becoming doctors, scientists, teachers, builders, even great leaders and we become them.

We imagine having a new car, a refrigerator, attaining the ability to fly and our reality accommodates what we imagined.

Yet, we still do not understand that to have a world that lives in peace, all we have to do is imagine it into reality.

Imagine a world that does not have a monetary system. A world that plays an entirely different game.

A world that has the single common goal of ensuring that humanity will thrive!

Imagine a world where there is no such thing as poverty.

Imagine a world where we build things to last so that we don't spend most of our lives repeating the process of creating the same things over and over because they are designed to not last.

Imagine a world where we teach our children to manage the resources of the Earth instead of consuming them.

Imagine a world without hunger, a world without war, a world without greed.

Of all the great achievements of man the single greatest (World Peace) will be real when we imagine it to be so.

If all we ever imagine for ourselves is a world that is corrupt and evil then that is the world we will have. If we imagine that we live to work and consume then that is what we are stuck with.

We have to imagine that world peace is possible before we can have it. The amazing thing about imagining something is that as soon as you do, all sorts of ideas will pop up supporting the what you imagined. The possibility that you create will begin to fill with real substance and whatever you imagined takes on a life of its own.

I listen to the rhetoric of the politicians who over and over propose that they can lead our countries and that they have a solution to the most pressing issues. I can't help but utter "bull-crap" in my mind every time one of these big winded blowhards gets up to the podium. They are all spewing out the same tired old ideas that they have said for a long time. None of them is really thinking outside the box. All of them are seeking change from within the confines of the paradigm that we are currently in.

You cannot expect the very mentality that got us into the mess to come up with a creative and profound idea to get us out. It would be like asking a rigid conservative to start coming up with some great liberal ideas. Or asking a liberal to think conservatively.

Everyone seems to be thinking in terms of how to repair the system that is crumbling when they need to be thinking of an entirely new system!

The reason that our leaders are not thinking of shifting the paradigms is because the current paradigms are working for them.

Our choice for leadership is severely limited by how much money the candidates have to campaign. The only candidates that ever make it to the ballot either have money of their own or raise money by accepting bribes and favors from big corporations and the wealthy elite.

It is accepted that they lie about what they promise before they are elected and they lie once they become elected.

We do not hold our elected officials accountable for what they promise and what they deliver. In the past, news organizations would investigate and report on scandals unswayed by the possible threat of retaliation. They sought truth and transparency. Now most news agencies are but puppets owned and controlled by the very big money that they are reporting on. The wolf is the shepherd!

Part of the problem is that our attitude and beliefs are as resigned as our systems are corrupt.

As long as "we the people" are willing to accept that all politicians and government are corrupt, our politicians and government will continue to be corrupt.

A select few in the world are absolutely happy with the way things are. They have money and with money they have a great life opportunity at their command so why would they want to change that. It's like the farmer who owns many acres of land and has slaves working for him to till the land, plant the seed and harvest the crop so that he can make more money, buy more land and enslave more to work his land. Its a good deal for the farmer and he sees no need to change things.

The "New Game" is a description of a paradigm shift for how we live our lives. We are currently playing the "monetary consumerism" game of life that isn't working very well and will eventually lead to the destruction of humanity and Earth itself. Here is an analogy that may help you to visualize what our current paradigm looks like:

Imagine that you and the rest of humanity are traveling in a spaceship. You have limited resources on this spaceship and if those resources are not managed properly, you will not reach a new planet that will support life. You and your families will live on this space ship for 75 thousand years in order to reach your destination. New generations will be born and live the majority of their lives on this spaceship. When your destination is reached, the colonization of a new planet will begin ensuring the survival of the human race.

While on this spaceship a group of people announce that they are going to create a monetary system based on a heavy metal that they have a small stockpile of. They explain that the food and other resources that were once freely available to ensure the survival of everyone will now be available to those who possess enough of the heavy metal to purchase them. These are some big guys and most everyone is afraid of them. They want luxury over and above what everyone else has and they are willing to do whatever it takes to have it. You soon get the idea that you too must work for these bullies to collect the heavy metal.

The big guys are also offering that if you do not have enough of the heavy metal to purchase what you need, you can go into debt and even pass that debt to your children so you will have what you need.

Everyone on the spaceship must start working toward getting as much of this heavy metal as they can in order to live in comfort while on their journey. The more of this heavy metal you have, the better you and your family will live. Oh, and don't worry about those who are not as crafty, lucky or as fortunate as you with regard to obtaining the heavy metal. Some of them will surely starve after living out their lives as best they can and they and their families will be discarded.

Those with the heavy metal will gather up and secure all the resources available and employ those who have little or no heavy metal to create tools and luxury items with a planned obsolescence so that they will not last creating the need to throw them away, gather more resources and build more of the same. This will create a continual job opportunity for those who can and are willing to work for the heavy metal and also give them something to go further in debt to get. Meanwhile the limited resources are being depleted. Don't worry about that either because more raw resources can be gathered by taking apart pieces of the spaceship. Yes, yes, we all know that by destroying our spaceship in pursuit of the heavy metal is going to cause a disaster for everyone including those who have plenty of the heavy metal. We will deal with that unfortunate situation when we are forced to.

Now, let's elect a body of people that under the guise of representing the will of the people to govern all of this. Oh, and the only people that have even a remote chance of being elected are those who have more of the heavy metal than what they need or can serve as puppets for the bullies.

Those elected officials will also control the laws and the law enforcement for the entire spaceship population ensuring that the system created stays intact. However, they will promise to squelch the fighting and unrest and make things more fair as people aboard the spaceship who are impoverished by the system fight, steal and kill in their efforts to obtain more of the heavy metal.

Instead of educating the children on how to manage the resources of the ship and creating a sustainable future, they will now be educated in the fine art of how to turn a profit and successfully compete with others for the heavy metal.

I think that everyone in the world regardless of age, ethnic heritage and social culture can clearly surmise what the most probable outcome of this scenario will be. In summary it would end something like this:

While many who cannot or are not willing to play this game simply die of starvation and despair, many others kill their fellow humans for their own personal gain. A few survive long enough to experience that their spaceship, now completely depleted of all resources is failing because of the way in which it was compromised for the pursuit of the heavy metal. And there they sit. Too late to do anything about it, disaster and the end of humanity is at hand.

But, they have a bunch of the heavy metal and their life experience as they die will be surrounded by the very greed that extinguished them and their fellow humans.

Over time people are born into monetary consumerism and it becomes a way of life that is really not questioned. When it is questioned, the person questioning is often discouraged by their peers as well as the establishment because they are potentially jeopardizing the perceived security and way of life others have become accustomed to. Many have even become dependent on the paradigm through a welfare system or direct employment by the governing body and are too afraid of losing that which they are dependent upon.

At some point, the heavy metal that once was a tangible is now strictly symbolic. The monetary system in place is merely a number tracking system that represents the wealth and debt used to control the masses.

The game on the spaceship changed from having a good life experience to a "monetary consumerism" game where control and selfish greed ruled.

The game we are playing on Earth is exactly what I just described in simplistic terms. The beautiful Earth is our spaceship complete with limited resources. Every second of every day we are playing the game of collecting as much of the heavy metal as we can at the expense of others and at the great peril of the very spaceship on which we live.

This is not so much about money as it is about control.

Money and the monetary consumerism paradigm is a method of control. The guys that took over the spaceship and the elite who are in charge on Earth really have no more use of the heavy metal than we have. They want to control the masses and the money game is their method!

The sad and most disturbing part of this reality is that we are born into this ridiculous game of a monetary consumerism system that has been in play for so long that we don't even know that it is a game and that we can and should change this game.

We in fact, MUST change the game to ensure the very survival of our species and the planet!

Chapter 3 – We Are ALL Slaves

I refer to the paradigm that we are living in as "the game" we are playing. In the game that we are born into we don't often take the time or have the inclination to consider what would happen if we completely shifted the paradigm. It simply doesn't occur to us or even if it does, it seems so insurmountable that we don't often give it real consideration.

We have to consider that the life we were born into is all about money. Plain and simple, the world revolves around money and everything else in life is second to that. Oh sure there are exceptions to that ideal but really, if we are completely honest, its all about money.

Ironically, the single greatest obstacle for achieving world peace is "MONEY". Look at it for what it is...

Money = debt

If you were to hold a dollar bill in your hand, you may think that this dollar represents a very small but real physical fraction of gold that is held in a safe place like "Fort Knox" that is owned by the people of the United States of America. That thinking is incorrect! Printed U.S. Dollars only represent a small fraction of what is supposed to be in circulation. And, the total amount of gold and silver held doesn't even come close to representing the reserve. Why? And more importantly, "why does this matter?" It matters because we are playing the money game and we need to understand that money is a completely made up aspect of the game of life.

In the United States, when our government decides that we need more money, they then go to the Federal Reserve Bank which is PRIVATELY OWNED by the wealthiest people on Earth and borrow the money. The Federal Reserve Bank gives our government what amounts to a promissory note representing the debt (plus interest). So... the dollar bill that you hold in your hand literally represents debt.

Woodrow Wilson signed the federal reserve act into law in 1913 in return for the support of the wealthiest, most influential men in the world during his presidential bid.

"Our great industrial nation is controlled by its system of credit. Therefore all of our activities are in the hands of a small group of men who chill and check true economic freedom. We have come to be one of the worst ruled, completely controlled and dominated governments in the world. No longer a government of the majority but a government of the opinion and duress of a small group of dominant men."

  — *Woodrow Wilson*

Debt = in-servitude

When you are in debt as is nearly every nation on Earth, then you are in-servitude until that debt is satisfied. The trouble is that the National debt for not only the United States but nearly all other nations on the planet is so great that it is mathematically impossible to ever pay it back. Again, you may ask "why is it impossible to pay the debt back?". The answer is that we are paying interest on that debt. The debt, combined with the interest being charged is accumulating at a more rapid rate than what can be paid back.

Many of us do not understand the numbers. We throw around the numbers like millions, billions and trillions as if they were all the same without a true appreciation for what these numbers are.

Just to give you some perspective, lets look at the numbers.

If you spent a dollar every second of every day, it would take you about 11.5 DAYS to equal 1 million.

If you spent a dollar every second of every day, it would take you about 31 YEARS to equal 1 billion.

If you spent a dollar every second of every day, it would take you about 30,000 YEARS to equal 1 trillion.

As of the writing of this book, the official United States deficit is roughly 15.8 TRILLION dollars.

You can see the United States debt accumulate live by visiting: http://www.usdebtclock.org/

And where in the world did this debt come from? The federal reserve was conceived by a group of the wealthiest people in the world in 1912. Why did our government feel as though we needed to have this organization to borrow money from? Did our country not have enough gold and material wealth to print its own money for the cost of the paper instead of paying interest on someone else's money?

Nearly all other nations on Earth are in a similar debt situation and because the United States dollar is the world reserve, we are all in the same boat so to speak!

Therefore, nearly every nation on Earth has a debt that can never be paid back and is in-servitude to whomever is holding that debt.

Now, the question is... "Who is holding that debt?". The answer is: "The very wealthy few who own the banks."

In-servitude = slavery

The monetary consumerism paradigm enslaves everyone except the very wealthy whom we are all in debt to. Oh you may say; "I'm not a slave, I have freedom". And you do have some freedom. The key word is "Some." If you were kept in shackles tied to a tree, you would not be very productive and therefore not be of much use to your master. However, if you are free to roam and you have the prospect of someday being able to enjoy retirement, you will be much more willing to work the majority of your life away.

The point is that if you want even a small chance of having a great life experience in the current monetary consumerism paradigm, then you better have money. Because without money, you are going to have less freedom than you would if you had it.

Here is a link to a great example of what we are talking about: http://www.wimp.com/withoutcrying/

This is a compelling speech at the 2003 U.S. Comedy Arts Festival by: Anthony Griffith.

Anthony describes how while struggling to get his career as a comedian off the ground, he had the opportunity to go on national television and how he had to create new material and be funny in order to make a living. He describes how he struggled to be funny and make up more funny material because this year in his life was his "big break." If he failed, then his career would fail leaving him without a much needed income to support his family. The tragedy is that during the year of his "big break" while going on national television to make money

for his family by being "funny," his newborn child was
battling and dying of cancer.

He had "some" freedom in that he could have turned
down the big breaks that came his way. But doing so
would surely mean that he and his family would suffer
monetarily. He had to be funny even as his child lay
dying in a hospital. - Still think that we are not slaves?

Most of us in the United States can relate to Anthony
Griffith as we have to go to work even in the midst of
crisis at home or even when we are really too sick or too
tired to do so.

How about the millions of children around the world
who should be playing with dolls and riding bicycles who
are instead, mining diamonds, making shoes or begging
in the streets for a little money just to live another day?

There are other ways that monetary consumerism
enslaves us all even if you individually have money.

If you have money, you are often doing all that you can
to keep it. You have to be aware of and skeptical of
everyone who has access to your fortune. Nobody can
really be trusted. Even making new friends and forming
new relationships can be next to impossible. When you
have money, you are a target for many who will want
you to part with it. The cage that you build for yourself
may well be one of luxury but it is still a cage!

What stands in the way of curing disease, providing food for the worlds hungry or making sure that every person on Earth has clean drinking water? We have the technology to cure the diseases, we have the food and about 70 percent of the surface of the Earth is water. What is in the way is money. This is a plain and simple truth that affects world peace at its core and it "is" the greatest threat to humanity.

Most crimes are committed and people imprisoned because people want money and will do whatever it takes to get it. Whether driven by need or greed, the end goal is the same.

Prior to the idea of money, the world operated largely on a barter system. People would trade what they had for what they did not have. The trouble with the barter system is that it was often difficult to determine the real value of the traded items.

Even with the invention of money it is still sometimes difficult to determine the value of something because the value is often determined by circumstance. For instance, if you were literally dying of thirst in the desert and you had a pocket full of gold, you would certainly trade all of your gold for a canteen of water.

When I was a young boy, I would ask my father's advice when it came to buying things. I would say something like, "Is this worth $10 Dad?" His reply would often be, "its only worth is what its worth is to you".

His advice stuck with me and sure enough, that is the best way to govern the value of anything...its only worth is what its worth is to you.

I have often wondered about the nature of mankind being greedy. The idea of money and trading something for something else in consideration of ownership is as old as humanity itself. There are however, cultures around the world that have defied these concepts and simply share all things among each other without the consideration of ownership. Among these were some American Indian cultures. Throughout the world there are still some cultures that simply share for the greater good of all. If someone needs something, they have but to ask for it and their needs are met to the extent of the ability of the community to provide.

You have no doubt heard the expression "you can't take it with you" when referencing death and material wealth. The concept of actually owning something is shattered when you die. We all come into this world with nothing and we leave the same way that we came. So, do we ever really own anything?

We are all living on borrowed time and using borrowed things. This is fact. Even if you argue that things can be passed on to family and friends, the fact is that there is no guarantee that they will get or retain what they got and when they die, they will leave it all behind just as you did.

To really get a perspective that will assist you here, you have to think in terms of your mortality. It also would be helpful to understand what we humans are.

Most of us believe that when we die, our spirit will leave our physical body and move on to a better place. This belief is common throughout nearly every religion on Earth.

So... logic would dictate that we are an energy or spirit being inhabiting a physical body. With that thought in mind... It is easy then to understand that it serves absolutely no purpose whatsoever to accumulate more than what we can use while we are temporarily occupying a physical existence!

We are an energy or spirit being that has the ability and privilege of occupying a physical existence. As such, we are playing a game that was already in motion before we got here. That does not mean that we have to keep playing this game! We are fully capable of transforming our world by playing a different game.

There is nothing wrong with having comforts and pleasure while we are here unless of course it is at the expense of others who are going without. And guess what? Many are going without in the world so that we can have the comforts and live in excess.

If you think that what you have is not at the expense of another then you are delusional! We could completely eliminate starvation in the world today if we just gave up purchasing gifts for one year in the United States at Christmas time.

That is just one year! A few powerful and wealthy countries in the world live like royalty compared to majority of the world population. Of course it is at their expense.

My point here is not to make you feel bad about having comforts in your life while others go without. I too am living a very privileged life and have more than I need. And, I'm not just picking on the Christian religion. We could feed the starving by giving up buying shoes for 1 year.

The point is that as long as others do not have what they need to survive, those of us who have more than we need are living at their expense.

We are not always conscious to these things because we are born into the game and the game itself does not encourage equality.

The paradigm that we live and have lived in for thousands of years is one based on the concept of ownership, selfish regard and entitlement. The vehicle for this paradigm is money.

The goal of the life game that the whole world is playing is to have MORE MONEY! We trade our bodies for it, we trade our time for it, we trade our health and happiness, our freedom and our dignity. We may very well be willing to trade the survival of humanity for it!

As long as the world chooses to keep playing the monetary consumerism game, the world will not be at peace because this monetary consumerism model is corrupt by nature and is counter to the law of equality.

When making money is the goal, the health and well being of others are compromised by greed and corruption. Look at the way the corporations are set up. Their goal is not to build the finest product for longevity and functionality. Their goal is to build the finest product for the greatest profit possible. It is widely accepted that this is the reason businesses are in business. The pursuit of this goal is often at the expense of the health and well being of human beings. By law, corporations must endeavor to make a profit!

Human beings are valued for their productivity. It is no different than when slavery was openly acceptable and you picked the youngest most physically productive slaves to work your fields and factories. You would feed, clothe and shelter them to keep them healthy enough to produce for you. The very young would be indoctrinated into the slavery mentality from their birth so that they would be obedient and the old would be discarded because their usefulness had diminished.

Isn't that exactly what we do now? We ARE the slaves!

Our children are taught to conform and obey at a very young age. They are not encouraged to question and explore. They are taught what to think instead of being taught how to think for themselves. They are told to think about what they want to be when they grow up. As if they could only be one thing when they grow up.

Human nature is not to become one thing. Human nature is to have many desires and when you find one thing that you are passionate about then, you would pursue that desire. Perhaps you would find that the one thing remained your passion. And so whats wrong with the idea that along the way, you discovered something else that was even more exciting based on the experience that you had to that point?

In monetary consumerism, it doesn't make sense to work that way because while that may suit our ability to thrive, it is not as efficient and profitable.

We often think that we have freedom of choice when it comes to our career and education. Sometimes we argue that in the United States, if a person is willing to work hard enough and long enough, that they can achieve anything. While this concept has been proven true and there are some great stories of exceptional people who had modest beginnings and achieved great success.

The question that we have to ask ourselves is; "What if everyone had the opportunity for great success without having to overcome such adversity?" Wouldn't we have many more great successes? After all, everyone who has something great to contribute may not have the strength and tenacity to make it to a point where they can contribute.

So, what if we could choose to spend our time and effort in the vain of our passion instead of deciding on our vocation based on the cost of the education. What if we didn't have to consider how we could make enough money to live on in that occupation?

The sad truth about our current enslavement is that we don't even know that we are slaves so we don't think to choose something different. The thought is never even on our radar!

There are mainly 3 scenarios for the functional description of our enslavement, at least in most industrialized countries.

1. You get student loans or spend a significant part of your acquired wealth to obtain your education for which now you are indebted. You work to first pay off the educational debt or recoup your

investment and then work as though that is the only choice you have because you made the decision to have a career doing that. You make great money, save for retirement and have everything you want and need. You are in the 1% of the worlds wealth and be it through luck, intelligence, hard work or perseverance, you feel like you are free and you wonder what is all this talk about our being slaves?

In this scenario, you are quite likely to have missed the fact that you have had multiple failed relationships with your wives, kids, family and friends. Or perhaps you have spent so much time focused on your profitable carrier that you have not managed to even form significant relationships.

How often do we see someone very successful in their career is miserable? We sometimes look in disbelief at what we think should be the greatest life of wealth and privilege as it self-destructs in front of all the world.

As of the writing of this book, there are over 400 billionaires in the United States. Many of these billionaires spend their time and effort to make the world a better place. They help the poor, create job opportunity, and are very benevolent toward others who are not as fortunate as they.

This is like a slave who has achieved preferred status with their master and is now treating the other slaves better. It is a great gesture but it doesn't fix the problem.

A "slave" is a slave. You can color it however you want. There are degrees of freedom for those who are more fortunate to play the game better. There is more freedom for those who are born into wealth. But living life in the paradigm, we are all slaves regardless of our standard of living.

2. You decide not to purchase a higher education and you end up doing what may be called: "blue collar" work in a factory, as a carpenter or truck driver. Now, given the ever rising cost of living you work most of the time just to maintain a living until you are too old, too tired or too broken to work anymore and you retire to a way of life that at best is comfortable as long as nothing major goes wrong financially.

   You may have also decided to enter the military as I did because I felt that I could not afford the education in any other way and it would give me the opportunity to experience the world and serve my patriotic obligation at the same time. The 99% of our military are made up of poor and middle class. This is by design not accident.

Coming from a "blue collar" family, I can tell you that our life was a just enough challenge to keep us struggling but not enough challenge to discourage our efforts. Compared to much of the world our standard of living was great. We always had food, water and shelter.

We also always had our eye on the opportunity to make a better life for ourselves. There was hope that someday we would live the "American Dream." What we didn't know is that our life was already "dreamy" compared to the standard of living in many parts of the world.

This is the genius of the modern slave paradigm. Its like having a carrot on a stick in front of you, just out of reach. You keep running toward it as fast as you can and sometimes it is within reach. Once you get a little taste of it, you chase even harder for the possibility of more!

3. You are one of the less fortunate who do not fit with what is defined as employable. Maybe you are physically or mentally challenged or maybe you just couldn't find the money and opportunity to explore a vocation of your desire. Now, you are dependent on the master that provides you the bare minimum to survive. It is just good enough where you are not suffering in your financial cage so badly that you must get out.

And, you are afraid to even try to do something for yourself because you may lose what little you have and further fall into poverty.

I once had a conversation on this "slavery" subject with a fellow who proclaimed his disagreement on the basis of his own situation. He said: "I'm not a slave" and went on to tell me that he had his home paid for, his cars paid for and he had enough money in the bank to live comfortably for the rest of his life. I acknowledged his accomplishment because it is not easy even in the United States to achieve this. I then recalled for him the 40+ years of hard work it took for him to get to this point. I asked him if he enjoyed his work enough to say that he traded his time wisely for it. I also asked him if he thought that he had accomplished his goals at the expense of others in any way. And then, I said, "So... that is great for you and how are your two children?" "Are they as comfortable as you?" "Are they working the job that they love and are passionate about in order to put food on the table, cars in the garage or to pay their mortgage?"; "And what about the people that you attend church with, are they all as fortunate too?"

You see, in this situation certain slaves that learn to play the game better may get a more luxurious standard of living.

That is like having a boat full of life jackets for yourself in an ocean while friends and family are drowning all around you!

What if you were doing great financially but then you or your family suffered a catastrophic health issue and it took everything you had tucked away just to survive?

I think back on the 1983 comedy "Trading Places" where Dan Aykroyd's character who is at the top of his game is quickly and cruelly put on the street by his bosses and replaced by Eddie Murphy's character who was living on the street. Money was the motivation for both characters. One character had been born into wealth and privilege while the other had been born into poverty. The theme of the movie was based on a bet between two wealthy brothers who owned the company that Dan Aykroyd's character worked for. The bet was to find out whether a person off the street could take the place and be as successful as the person that was groomed for the job.

Having money gives a person access to education, healthcare and a plethora of opportunities.

But, it doesn't take much for someone with more money and more power than you or an unfortunate circumstance to knock you down to a mere existence.

Another way to look at it is even more concerning to me. You may become the master slave who enslaves others!

Do you own a business where people work for you? Do you can dictate what they can and can't do holding their wages over them to get what you want so that your business can be profitable?

I have owned and still own a small business (at the time of writing this book). I am thankful on one hand that I can provide employment and a good working environment. On the other hand I am disgusted that I am part of the slavery paradigm to the degree that I use others to become more profitable.

In many parts of the world, you may have to provide everything from sexual favors to risking your life to keep your job. In many cultures there are supposed to be laws to protect you from abuse but we all know how employment really works and how money corrupts!

It wasn't long ago that we didn't even have child labor laws or laws that protected against sexual or ethnic discrimination in the United States.

No matter what society you are in and how many laws you have, the nature of the money system is such that there is always corruption!

Whether you are a slave working for someone or you are the slave employing slaves, you are still a slave because you are part of the paradigm that enslaves!

And what about the elderly slaves? In many cultures, the old, feeble and weak, are simply discarded by system.

In the United States, we have found it profitable to keep our old people alive as long as possible!

Our healthcare has become industrialized for huge profit. We now have a vested interest in poor health and the treatment of symptoms related to poor health. In the United States, getting old means spending a great deal of time getting healthcare treatments that are enormously expensive.

If you don't have the ability to pay, then the cost will be shared by all who contribute to the social security and welfare systems. So... enslavement of the elderly is very profitable.

We work hard and the hard work both mentally and physically take their toll. We eat fast because we don't have time to eat properly. The fast food and even the non-fast food often does not offer the nutrients that human beings need to be healthy. It often is actually very unhealthy. Many creditable studies have been published that directly link the top diseases to poor diet. Not to mention that the chemicals and genetic engineering that are used to grow the livestock for our food in the name of making more profit are toxic to us.

Why would our society allow this? Because it is profitable for us to be sick. The industrial healthcare business is making a bunch of money off the cycle of bad and toxic nutrition.

Humanity is surely coming to the conclusion that something is wrong. The trouble is that most who correctly perceive that something is wrong are trying to change what they perceive is wrong (treating the symptom).

Treating the symptom is not addressing the cause of what is wrong.

Take our welfare system in the United States for instance. What is not working is that people who do not function in a working society for one reason or another whether self-imposed or not should have their basic need for food, shelter and healthcare met. However, once people become dependent on the assistance they receive, they are not provided a clear attainable path to become self-sufficient again. In fact, they become entrapped by the very system that is assisting them!

Not only do they become entrapped, but so do all the "greed" systems that depend on their entrapment. By "greed" systems I mean the systems that thrive and depend on people being impoverished such as healthcare, groceries, farms, and so called sin commodities.

More often than not, a person who is not able to take care of themself and their family become depressed and resigned to a life of minimums. They lose hope, dignity and become victim to the system that is providing their assistance.

If a person is on welfare or SSI for disability, they don't have the means to support their need for proper nutrition. This often leads to poor physical and mental health that supplies the all too eager healthcare money making machine with a steady supply of revenue to treat the illnesses of those on welfare. They not only treat those who are dependent on the treatment but they themselves become dependent on the revenue that is generated by providing the treatments. The cycle perpetuates itself!

People who cannot or people who choose not to earn a viable living by producing enough product or service to generate income to sustain them, become a product in the system themselves. The system actually needs them to become ill, and dependent!

Others become dependent on the system through employment. They take up jobs with the controlling governing body. They are not going to look for solutions or ways to change the system because this is the system that provides for their livelihood.

The workforce employed by the controlling governing body is encouraged to grow because it provides a larger base of dependent minions that will keep the controls in place and continue to ensure our enslavement.

War is a hugely profitable part of our enslavement. World banks profit by funding both sides of the wars. And then they profit more by the reconstruction of the very cities that they funded the destruction of, placing further debt and enslavement on the human beings who live there. Wars are very profitable!

The genius of many of the wars we fight today is that many of the wars we are fighting are "ghost wars." "Ghost wars" such as "the war on drugs" or "the war on terrorism" are even more profitable because they are endless and funded based on the successful propaganda in the form of fear campaigns. We are all willing to pay what ever it takes to keep the boogie man from getting us!

What better way to keep the money flowing with the blessing of the general population for an indefinite time? Do you see the difference between a war that is legally declared on a finite tangible such as another country versus a war that is declared on an intangible group of people?

We have spent billions and billions of dollars fighting "ghost wars" and if you just use the "war on drugs" as an example you will find that not only has the war cost us billions of dollars but it has also failed miserably! Yet the war is profiting the banks and the people who own them so the "ghost wars" rage on.

The same is true for the war on terrorism. We have spent over a trillion dollars on this relatively new war. Tens of thousands of lives have been lost and the world is arguably less safe today than it has ever been.

It is all about dominating whomever is deemed a threat by the richest in the world so that the profits may keep flowing.

For a minute, just take a deep breath and see how all of this fits and supports monetary consumerism.

Normally in the United States, the president would have to obtain congressional approval in order to go into another country and start dropping bombs, sending in troops and killing people. There would be a whole series of events that would have to be done in order to allocate the tax payer funds that would be used to fund such a war. But, as continuing part of "the war on terror", many of the processes and approvals are bypassed.

We are all financing the "ghost wars" and most of the time we have no clue who is being killed and where the money is going.

Where does the money come from when our National debt is at an all time insurmountable high? Well, it comes to our government in the form of loans from the Federal Reserve Bank. It is debt which is shared by citizens of the world, because the United States dollar has long been the world reserve. Most of the world is unknowingly financing the "ghost wars"! Meanwhile the debts continue to grow and as I have said; "debt" = slavery!

This "negative financing" situation is not unique to the United States. Where are the countries borrowing the money from to bail them out of their financial crisis? They are borrowing money from banks in other countries that are also in debt!

None of it makes any sense. The monetary consumerism paradigm is falling apart, will not and cannot sustain a thriving humanity.

As the population on Earth grows, what do you think happens to the value of human life?

For example, if you had a large farm and 50 slaves to run this farm efficiently for you then each slave has a value. But, what value do you have for each slave if there are 100 and you only need 50?

Why do we not feed the 15 million children who are dying of starvation every single year when we have food rotting in silos?

Why do we spend trillions of dollars to fight wars instead of spending that money to figure out how to solve the problems that create disparity in the first place?

Because the minority who control the money don't value human life as much as they value money! It is not profitable to end the starvation of human beings and it is very profitable to fight wars.

It's the truth and it's ugly!

The enslavement of humanity is not a new idea or something that just happened. It may or may not even be a conspiracy. Whatever the original intention, it has long been exploited by those who seek to profit at the expense of others.

It is a system that is serving a very small part of humanity very well and we keep it alive out of fear, complacency and ignorance.

Chapter 4 – Time for World Peace

There are as many ideas and opinions about how to achieve world peace as there are people. In this time of unparalleled global uncertainty about our economy, social and political futures, we are a world in need of guidance. There is no question that we are facing a global crisis that will challenge humanity like never before!

Here is just one possible scenario of how the world could change for the worse in the near future:

1. Global climate change and changes in our ecological systems caused by unchecked man made pollution creates catastrophic disasters around the word.
2. The world economy continues to degrade until total collapse of the monetary system.
3. More wars will be fought for need and greed leaving even more of the population destitute.
4. Without funding and resources, disease will spiral out of control killing millions.
5. Nuclear weapons will be used further creating stress on the world environment.
6. Even the countries with the most wealth will suffer great hardships. When suffering, even the most civilized, privileged and best educated will resort to violence.

If you think that sounds scary, you have only to look around at some of the current dooms-day prophecies that are circulating in print and on the internet. It seems that on a global scale, everyone believes that something major is going to happen in the next year or two.

So... what do we do?

First, just for a moment, consider how we got to where we are. The paradigms that we currently live in evolved just as we humans have evolved over the Milenia. We have evolved separated by geography which caused us to develop very different cultures with very different perspectives. Some cultures have developed quickly and others more slowly. Some cultures have been content to live life according to tradition while others have chosen to live life in constant change. Pursuing bigger, better, faster and with an insatiable appetite for more!

In the beginning, we (the human race) did not get together to intelligently design a plan that serves the best interest of all humanity. And this is precisely where the problem is!

There is nothing wrong with how humanity developed, what has been suffered by the natural evolution of the diversity of perspectives has provided us with a pretty good idea of what works and what doesn't.

We also experienced life in billions of ways that we could not have otherwise experienced. For some reason, mankind often takes a pretty good beating before realizing a better way to do something. After all we are one of, if not "the" most stubborn creatures to ever exist on this beautiful planet. Humanity has changed the face of the entire Earth more in the past two hundred years than any creature in the 4 billion years before us!

It should be no mystery whatsoever how humanity got to where we are now. The mystery is why we continue to haphazardly evolve without consideration and consensus on where we are going!

We have to unite in our understanding that we are living life according to a model that is fundamentally flawed. Then, we must believe that we have the intelligence and tenacity to design a new model that works better for everyone.

We are not talking about rocket science here! All we have to do is know that we must shift the paradigm and be committed to make it happen.

When president John F. Kennedy said that he wanted the United States of America to go to the moon within a decade, many people including the scientist of the time thought that he was way too optimistic. But somehow, with the belief that it could be done and using less computing power than what is in a smart phone today, there we were landing on the moon.

It is that kind of passion and belief that we need in order to achieve world peace!

We must all become concerned and have a sense of urgency and determination. We must communicate with friends and family leveraging the Internet and other communications that will unite us in our vision and in our quest for freedom.

Are you are sick and tired of they way things are in the world, sick and tired of the same type of politicians telling you that they have the answers only to find out things are worse than ever?

Are you are sick and tired of working a job that you don't like just to barely support a family that you never get to see because you are working too much to enjoy them?

Are you are tired of knowing that 15 million children die in the world every year while there is enough food to feed them?

Are you are sick and tired of trillions of dollars being spent on wars instead of solving the problems that have lead to the discontent?

If the list goes on and on for you as it does me, then take note because now you can help to achieve world peace!

You can start by having conversations with your friends and family and bring up some of the points that I have mentioned in this book.

To achieve world peace, we have to begin talking about the paradigms so that others recognize that the paradigm we are currently living is what is in the way of world peace. We all have to start talking about our commitment to world peace and know that we can shift the paradigm and live by design.

We must believe in ourselves and love ourselves enough to know that we are the only ones that can bring about world peace.

Once we have a general understanding that there is a problem with monetary consumerism and that it will not allow for world peace, then we have a chance to do something about it.

The paradigm that we are living in was not designed. It evolved and became exploited.

If you were designing the world and how it should work would you design it the way that we are living it right now?

We can and will do better!

Chapter 5 – The "NEW" Game

If we really want to achieve "world peace", then we have to shift the paradigm that we currently live in and play a new game!

As with all games we have to have an objective or main goal. It seems that we have been playing the game of life without a consensus of a main goal. Some have a goal to simply survive while others have goals of great wealth and luxury.

The diversity of perspectives ensure that the goals of every human being are different. If you take into consideration all the different perspectives. All the different goals and all the different rules of the game... Then, factor in the various social economic cultures and beliefs, you may quickly understand why the objectives of the game of life are different for everyone.

However, the objective to have more money so that you can have a better life is an almost universal goal. We have made this fictitious thing called "money" into something we perceive as real and valuable.

The truth is that "money" is only real and valuable because the game we are playing says it is! By placing our value on money, we lose sight of what really matters.

The "NEW GAME" is placing the ultimate value on human beings so that we can survive, thrive and have a great life experience!

If money is not being used as a vehicle to our ability to survive or thrive, then nothing is is the way for us to survive and thrive.

Humans are meant to thrive in life. Not just survive! If we could all agree that "money" is what is in the way of our having a great life experience then, we may work more diligently to shift the paradigms and play a new game.

The best way for me to express the new game and appeal to you is through simple logic. It is difficult to argue with logic!

The logic looks like this:

1. Human beings cannot survive or have a good life experience without other humans –If you are the only one surviving, the human race would die out. Also people need people to interact with in order to have a good life experience. We literally need each other!

2. Humans want to thrive! –this is why we survive. If there were absolutely no hope of enjoying life and you knew for certainty that your life would be miserable would you really want to live? We need to thrive!

3. Humans have a need to understand their place in the world –We would not be able to thrive if we had no purpose. We all want to be accepted and valued. We need purpose!

Therefore the objective of the game of life is to have a good life experience by ensuring that other humans survive and thrive because your good life experience depends on it! And, you must have a reason for living too so you need purpose.

The logic further expanded –We have the need to have others in our life for reproduction but also because we humans only know who we are by sharing ourselves with others. If you had a luxurious life with everything you could want but you had nobody to share it with, then you would find yourself alone and miserable.

What is the point of surviving if your life is miserable? Therefore survival by itself is not enough motivation to sustain the human race. That is why we must not only survive but we need to thrive.

Also, if you had others to share life with. And, you personally were not miserable, but the others were all miserable. Would you feel as though you could thrive?

If you were surviving and you were not alone but you had no purpose, then why would it matter that you survive? Have you ever noticed that when you have no purpose, time has no meaning for you? Purpose is what creates the opportunity to thrive!

It sounds simple because it is simple. It is also logical!

This logic dictates that you cannot get what you want at the expense of others because you are undermining your own objectives. Instead, you must work in cooperation with others in order to achieve your mutual objectives.

Are you familiar with the laws of robotics as introduced by Isaac Asimov in 1942 to govern robotic behaviors?

While we have not yet seen robots sophisticated enough to interact with us every day socially, the laws of robotics have been widely debated anticipating that the day will come where we will be interacting with them. The laws of robotics are:

1. A robot may not injure a human being, or, through inaction allow a human being to come to harm.
2. A robot must obey the orders given it by human beings except where such orders would conflict with the First Law
3. A robot must protect its own existence as long as such protection does not conflict with the First or Second Law.

Similarly, we could come to a very basic understanding and consensus that would govern the behaviors of humanity.

If made to be laws, the three laws of humanity would look like this:

1. **Humans must ensure that others survive and thrive**
2. **Humans must themselves seek to survive and thrive without violating the first law**
3. **Humans must seek purpose without violating the first or second laws**

I'm going to coin the phrase referring to the 3 points of logic as: "Human Law". If we could design how robots should live and interact with humans, then why wouldn't we design life for ourselves?

Note that when Isaac Asimov conceived his design for robotic behavior, he did not say that they should be mainly concerned with being profitable and earn as much money as they could at the expense of human beings and other robots!

While there are billions of complexities that can be added and modified, the three main laws hold true and will ensure the survival of the human species.

It is essential that we all understand this basic logic! The very survival of our species depends on it.

Now, if you can accept that the universal goal of the game of life is to play by making sure that everyone survives and thrives and everyone has a good life experience... Then, let's look at the current game goals that we are playing by and see the differences in the paradigms.

In the current paradigm, we are experiencing life literally scrounging for food, water and shelter or we are experiencing life to have more money. There is little in between.

If we already have the basic need of food, water and shelter covered then we are likely playing the money game. In the money game, we acquire more at the expense of others and at our own expense by consuming our limited resources. Eventually we deplete our resources and we are left with money. But without resources we have no need for money because we can't produce anything to spend our money on.

The simplified cycle where people with money profit from people without money looks something like this:

1. People without money to mine resources from the Earth so that we can use those resources to make things for consumption.
2. People without money labor to manufacture consumibles that have a "planned obsolescence"

3. People without money to labor to stock store shelves with the limited lifespan things.
4. People without money then have earned enough money to purchase the limited lifespan consumibles putting more money into the pockets of the people who already have money.
5. The cycle repeats over and over as long as the resources last.

In their quest for more, people with money have recently and unwittingly shot themselves in the foot.

Many manufacture's have either replaced the people without money that used to work in their production/sales cycle with automated machines and robots or with people with even less money in more impoverished countries. What they didn't factor into their planning is that the people that used to do the work for them and consumed their things, now do not have jobs and therefore cannot purchase the things that are being produced! And the people who produce at even lower wages, still cannot afford to buy their things because they are so poor and use all the money that they earn just to survive!

In the current game the goal is to have more at the expense of others who do not have enough. The resources are limited but those who want more will build limited lifespans for all they produce ever ensuring the demand for their things (planned obsolescence).

This is a very small and simplified part of the problem with the current game but it serves as an example for the difference in what the game could and must move toward.

In the "NEW GAME" we would take the limited resources into consideration and produce things that last for as long as possible.

If we are not concerned about making more money, we would produce only as much as the real demand dictates.

The workers who produce the product would look for ways to increase efficiency and reduce energy consumption. There would be no single entity benefiting at the expense of others, the benefit would be for all who need the product.

When you take money out of the equation, you produce with real purpose and intelligence!

Advancement in various technologies also deflate the old game paradigm because as we automate production, we have less need for human labor. Production efficiency increases beyond the demand, products last longer and profitability declines.

Technology will reduce and eliminate the need for certain medicines. Technology is currently held back by monetary limits. Just think of what can be accomplished if we were to allow research and development to flourish without monetary concern!

You may be inclined to argue that if we took away the money incentive that everyone would go on vacation or stay home and play video games. There would be no reason to work if everything was provided. People would be all too happy to let someone else do the work while they did nothing. This may be true for some. It certainly is true for some in our current paradigm.

However, consider what the world would look like if we built everything to last for as long as it could. If we were not in the money game which is driven by consumption, we could build things once or make them extensible and therefore work much less to achieve the same results of supply and demand.

Think of it! We could have things that lasted virtually forever and only have to make more to keep up with growing population or other logical demand. We would work considerably less without compromising anything!

In the current game, we work 5 to 7 days a week needing every penny of 2 incomes per household just to consume product that will inevitably break or be outdated sometimes even before it is paid for!

Here are just some examples of how the current game stunts progress, wastes resources and is utterly absurd.

1. We have built automobiles for over a century. They are priced so that they rust or give out about the time that they are paid for and it's time to repeat the cycle. Could we make them so they don't rust out or give out? Of course we can. We have had the technology for years. There are thousands and probably millions of products that are built in a similar limited life cycle. - It's all about money

2. Cancer is one of the leading causes of illness and death. There have been many promising and proven cures. I personally know several people in my small circle of friends and family that have suffered and/or died from one form of cancer or another. Are the cures available to us? Well, through expensive and exhaustive treatments some cures are available. How on Earth would the big pharmaceutical companies and the insatiable healthcare industries continue to amass their great wealth if the cures were made available? - It's all about money

3. Do you know that so called "zero-point" energy was discovered over a hundred years ago? This free and clean energy has been rediscovered many times only to be snuffed out by the big

energy companies to protect their interests!
"Zero-point" or FREE energy is found
throughout the universe. It is abundant but if it
can't be metered, how can the big energy
companies make their trillions? - It's all about
money

I have to pause for a moment... Because you may be
thinking about the "new game" eliminating the need for
money and wondering; Is it socialism or communism?
Oh dear what have I gotten myself into?

It's none of that. It is a new paradigm. It's a "new
game" where the goal is **not** to have more of everything
at the expense of everyone including the Earth itself.

The "new game" is to ensure a good life experience for
everyone so that humanity will survive.

Most people don't even know what Socialism or
Communism are or the differences between them. I can
tell you that both are forms of government and both still
have currencies and debt. So in short, both are just
other methods of managing slavery.

The difference between what I'm talking about and any
currently defined social/political or government
philosophy is... I'm suggesting that we live our lives by
logical design and with the purpose of ensuring that
every human being has the ability to not only survive but
thrive!

The current game is similar to the Monopoly game. In the beginning of the game it is fun to roll the dice and see where chance may take you. But eventually, one player dominates the board. One player owns most of the property and has most of the money. Everyone else is just rolling the dice to see how long before they are finished.

In the end, you put all the hotels, all the houses and the money back into the box.

In the current game we are playing, the players who have most of the money and property simply let the other players back into the game.

They strip most of the world down to mere survival. They finance and incite wars. They bankrupt the people, foreclose on their homes and businesses and then give them just enough money back to entice them to keep playing. The cycle is repeated over and over.

Someone, in this case a select few have money and all they need and they are controlling the game.

Humanity cannot survive this game and the current paradigm. Money is a part of the game that was made up in order for the select few to control the masses.

The concept of money may have been a necessary part of our evolution. But think of it, if we all got our heads on straight, would we really be playing the money game?

Someone made up the money game and as easily as it was invented it can be tossed out.

In order to toss out the old paradigm, we need to define the basic needs of all human beings to have a foundation for a good life experience.

Again, it's not rocket science!

The goals and rules that we can define for a "NEW GAME" are simple and will provide for everyone.

Everyone needs food, water and shelter. Everyone needs to ensure that everyone else thrives. Everyone needs to thrive themselves and everyone needs purpose.

Chapter 6 – How Will Life Look?

The "NEW GAME" – We are on this beautiful spaceship called "Earth" and we are unified as a species to live our lives by design. We have given up the old "money" paradigm. We are devoted now to making sure that the whole of humanity has a great life experience.

Some of what I am going to describe to you in this chapter may sound like science fiction. Indeed some of what I am sharing is not possible today. However, I have researched many technologies and everything that I am describing with regard to technology is either here today or highly probable within the next decade.

If we adopt this "NEW GAME" paradigm, the development of all these technologies and even more are probable!

In the "NEW GAME" paradigm we manage our natural resources intelligently and responsibly. We create enough product to meet demand, recycle all that we use and endeavor to discover more efficient, longer lasting materials that are safe and effective. The goal is to make the best of what we have.

We still have disagreements, infidelity, mental illness, power hungry people and a myriad of other issues to contend with. However, the solutions are created and delivered with intent to solve not intent to profit. When profit is not a factor, we will create better resolutions for everything.

Without the worry and stress of money, we are happier, healthier and much of the discontent that leads to disagreements, infidelity, mental illness and insatiable hunger for power simply go away.

We work less, play more and we allow the creativity of human beings to flow without restriction! Technology flourishes, health issues are reduced dramatically and we discover that we are more alike in the world than we are different.

Millions more humans are alive now because they have food, water and shelter. They are bright, intelligent and they contribute to the world with ideas and production because they are able to thrive.

The cry of hungry children is never heard and everyone works in cooperation to achieve advances in every aspect of science, technology, spirituality and functionality.

Conservation of all natural resources contributes to the overall health of the Earth.

In the past, virtually every species of animal on Earth were on the decline. Now many species are making a recovery.

Let's look at the specific areas of the world that are unrecognizable.

Education – We now teach our children to question everything. We encourage "free thinking" and totally new educational processes.

We look at the most effective methods around the globe of teaching the foundational and critical basics and we adopt, refine and improve.

Children that are more active by nature are not drugged to bring their level of energy down to suit the lower energy of others. Instead, the educators find ways to leverage that energy and stimulate them.

We no longer try to figure out how to profit by inventing things that will benefit the world. We no longer teach our children how to get a competitive edge by cloaking their discoveries or shrouding their ideas in secrecy. We instead teach them to share their ideas and knowledge openly and transparently. This approach results in a frenzy of cooperation and the exponential birth of many new ideas!

Teachers are rewarded for their excellence and are only limited by their creativity and ingenuity.

Money is no longer a limitation for anyone. Everyone can receive the education that they desire so more students are exposed to education that was once not possible.

Better educated people result in more scientific, technological and spiritual breakthroughs. The world advances at a rate never experienced in history!

We are able to manufacture any material we desire at any time so now many resources that were once finite are now infinite!

War is no longer a profitable business therefore, the outbreak of war is a rare and only occurs when someone is caught up in the old paradigm mentality. From time to time a dictator mentality pops up. Someone from the old game who cannot or will not make the transition. They find it difficult to gain support and momentum. The masses who see that the new paradigms are essential shut these people down quickly and work to teach them a better way.

Advances in molecular science have provided us with the ability to create any material substance we desire. Instead of melting a piece of metal and forming it for the desired purpose, we now design what we need and it is automatically manufactured from the molecule up!

Everyone has the ability to tell a computer what they want whether it be a steak or a new air conditioner for their home and in a matter of minutes to hours, it shows up in their molecular production machine. Does this

sound like science fiction to you? Look up scanning
tunneling microscopes and you will see that even today,
we can build virtually anything we desire at the
molecular level. Also, 3D printing which is a current
technology, will advance without limits for instant
creation of whatever we desire.

If money is not an issue the development of these
technologies will not be monopolized by the government
and dubbed "A national security interest".

Products are manufactured locally instead of the absurd
process of shipping material to a remote part of the
world and then using inexpensive slave labor to
manufacture the product and shipping it all the way
back to where the product is consumed. This localized
manufacturing is many times more efficient and saves
time, material and valuable resources.

*Nanotechnology is the technology based on the very
small. When I say "very small" I mean 1 billionth of a
meter! That is much smaller than a single blood cell.
This technology has been in development since it's
conception in 1959. You may not have heard of it but
nanotechnology is currently changing our world in
many wonderful ways.*

Utilizing nanotechnology in materials is now common.
You do not have to wash your clothing anymore because
the materials used for clothing are made with nano-

fibers that repel all liquids. You may have to shake them off once in a while but the days of washing and drying garments and materials are gone. This means that harmful soaps and cleaning chemicals are now obsolete. Water is better conserved and clothing lasts much much longer.

This same technology is used on buildings and homes keeping them shielded from natural and man made soiling. A wonderful secondary benefit is that the new materials are also fire proof, stronger and much more durable making them last longer!

Humans enjoy a happier healthier life style and many diseases simply go away because of the reduced stress.

Healthcare is now concerned more with prevention than treatment. The brilliant minds in this field are less burdened and have more time and energy to devote to effective prevention and treatments that were previously too expensive to pursue. Without financial limitations, research and development are producing astounding medicines and technological breakthroughs at unprecedented speed!

Our new global cooperation will result in sharing information freely. Patents are no longer needed and no longer keep great inventions from reaching and benefiting the world.

The advances in every area of life put us many years ahead of where we would have been in the old paradigm.

Because proper nutrition is now the focal point of producing food, better more nutritious food is produced. With better more nutritious food, the world becomes healthier and because the world is healthier, we produce better thinkers and better producers in every respect.

Something called the age of "conscious evolution" is at hand and we are experiencing life as if for the first time!

Aging is not only stopped but it is reversed! Now, you have the option to live as long as you desire and be as young as you wish.

Robots do all the undesirable labor throughout the world. People no longer put themselves in harms way because all the dangers are minimized. Production of food and manufacturing are largely carried out completely by robotics.

Homes are now as mobile and stationary as you wish. They are built out of carbon nano-fiber that makes them feather light and yet stronger than steel. With our anti-gravity generators, our homes are able to be parked above the surface of the Earth as well as on the surface.

With the exponential advances in technology, we are able to integrate nano-technology with our human physiology transcending our own mental and physical limitations. We are becoming super-humans!

Because money is no longer in the way, discoveries of Earth like planets are common and the technology needed to travel safely to these planets is being developed. Mankind is free to explore!

We now elect leaders based on their ability to lead instead of how much money they have to campaign. Government works better because leaders are there to lead without taking legal bribes through lobbyist. The leaders we elect are truly concerned with the best interest of everyone because that is human law and they understand that human law is essential to the survival and ability of humanity to thrive.

We are entering into a golden age of human evolution where our biggest problem is dealing with the incredible speed of change.

In "The New Game" EVERYONE wins and ALL of humanity thrives!

To some, this sounds idealistic. To that I say, "IT IS"! It is an idea that is ideal and why shouldn't it be? Why do we believe that we are meant to live in a world that is not ideal? What is the point?

The paradigm that we currently live in may have been created as much by chance as it was by design and conspiracy. It falls far short of what we human beings are capable of. For the first time in history, we have the global communications and intelligence to stop the madness and create the world exactly in a way which works best for everyone.

We are on this beautiful spaceship called "Earth" and we are suddenly AWARE! We are aware that the paradigm needs to shift and we need to play a new game so that we all can reach our destination in the universe!

In a decade, the world as we knew it has changed so dramatically that we are all nearly giddy with amazement!

In two decades, we have all but forgotten the ways of the past and when we do remember the old monetary consumerism paradigm, we laugh with disbelief that we once lived that way!

We vow to never repeat the past!

Chapter 7 – Transitioning (Our Greatest Challenge)

The transition from the "Old Game" to the "New Game" is likely to be our greatest challenge. So many have no idea what that could look like. We are programmed from the time we are born to believe in a way of life that was already set in place long before we showed up.

Think of how you got to where you are with your beliefs to this point in time. One day, you showed up in the world. The game of life was already in motion. The social, political, religious paradigms were already in place and depending on where and when you showed up, you simply were taught what those around you knew. That's how it works for everyone whether you showed up in on a farm in the mid-west of the United States or in the booming metropolis of Hong Kong, China.

You are programmed from birth to believe according to the time and place for which you are born. If those around you worship cows and aspire to thrive in a community that grows rice, then you will most likely worship cows and grow rice.

If you are born into wealth and most of those around you are educated and primarily concerned about money, then you are most likely to continue to be educated and be mostly concerned about money.

Because of where and when we are born we have certain beliefs. We sometimes get the notion that our beliefs are our own. We identify ourselves with those beliefs so strongly that we can't see that they are mostly a result of where and when we are born and we will fight fiercely to defend them.

This is the biggest hurdle that humanity must overcome! We have to understand that we believe what we believe largely because that is what we have been taught for most of our lives. We have to set aside our strongly held beliefs and be open to some new ideas. This is the first step in transforming our world and creating our life experience in the world by intelligent and intentional design.

To really transition into this "new game", we have to also realize how we are spending our lives in the current monetary game.

The very nature of the monetary consumerism paradigm is wasteful. We waste our time and precious resources to build things that will be consumed so that we can waste more time and more precious resources to replace them. The cycle is what keeps the money flowing.

Every facet of our lives is centered around keeping the money flowing.

In the United States, we wake up and rush to work between 8 and 12 hours a day, 5 to 7 days per week, 50 weeks per year, just to make enough money to keep up with the cost of living and all the while hopeful that we will somehow save a little for retirement.

Most of what we call "the industrialized world" has become very good at over producing and over consuming. We can't seem to get enough and it is all at the expense of the one thing we cannot get back... Our time and our lives.

We seldom talk to our neighbors or even our children because we are too busy. We have fast food that is nutritionally lacking and killing us faster.

We have more sickness because of the stress. We spend more money every year to combat the effects of the poor diet and stress so... We have to work harder and longer to earn the money that we need to keep living a life that we do not enjoy much.

So when we choose to play a new game and make the transition, the first thing on our agenda is to eliminate the money and the consumer mentality that has us all enslaved. This is a scary thought because everyone will ask: "what do we do now?".

To foresee everything that must take place and smooth out every conceivable detail is next to impossible. That being said, generally, not much would change at first.

We all would hold our current jobs to keep the wheels of production, distribution and service turning. The basics are especially important. We need food, water, shelter and energy. All jobs that are connected to the production and delivery of these basic needs must continue as we transition.

The jobs we will have no use for are related to money and control of money. This means that the banking jobs, the money creation jobs, the money manipulation jobs and all the jobs that exist only to serve the monetary paradigm are instantaneously obsolete.

At first we must give ourselves time to get used to the idea and set our goals to make a swift transition.

There will always be those who don't believe that the transition will happen.

Greed and fear will have some people trying to get more than they need and to obtain as much material possessions as possible. We must have a point system in place to allow tracking and rationing. We must rely on everyone to keep the three laws of humanity a priority for themselves and to promote this ideology to everyone.

There is plenty of everything for everyone and everyone's needs will be met. Everyone will almost instantly feel the relief of not having to pay a mortgage payment, car payment etc.

During the great depression of the 1930's the only thing that we really were short of was this made up thing called "money".

Businesses closed down while everything that they needed in terms of material was still available just like it had been in years past.

People went without food and shelter although there was plenty of food and shelter. Well, at least until farmers could no longer farm because they could not afford what they needed to run their farms.

The only thing that was really in shortage was "money". Nothing else vanished.

Once a couple of weeks pass in our transition, we will begin to set up routines and with clear minds at every level of our citizenship, we will structure a way of life that works naturally.

The greatest resistance will likely come from those global elitist who have tremendous wealth and believe that it is their place to control the rest of us. However, if they have no slaves to do their bidding, they will stand alone.

I'm not for one minute going to pretend to know all the best ways for humanity to make this transition.

I have ideas but this is where the brilliance of a collective and collaborative genius will come into play.

We have the great minds already working on the plan for how we can make this transition and literally millions of great ideas are already out there (please visit http://thevenusproject.com and http://zeitgeistmovie.com).

Your contribution can also be given at our website "http://thenewgame.org" and on Facebook.

I only intend to give you some of my ideas on how the paradigms can shift and what some of the possibilities are. Your genius is needed!

In our new paradigm everyone will have the opportunity to choose to contribute to the world in whatever area of interest that they are passionate about.

Because there are no monetary restrictions, people who have the aptitude for farming and love to farm will become farmers while people who have the aptitude and passion for medicine and healing will have unrestricted access to the education that will provide that way of life for them.

We often mistake money as being the motivator for progress. When in fact this is the case for some progress to be sure, it is not the motivation behind the greatest and most beneficial inventions. And just imagine for a second what progress could have come to humanity if it were not being held back by the confines of the present monetary system.

How many times have you or someone you know come up with a great idea for an invention only to be discouraged by the cost of seeking a patent or the cost of production? Billions of great inventions have not been brought to light because there wasn't enough money.

Still, billions more ideas and inventions were never even heard of because the brilliant minds that conceived them were too busy trying to survive to even consider sharing them with the world!

I like what Dr. Terry Jay van der Werff, CMC had come up with for the top 5 greatest inventions of the past 2,000 years:

1. **Indo-Arabic number system, including zero** - science is unthinkable without it.

2. **Waterworks** - clean water and waste disposal are more important for health than medicine.

3. **Printing press** - which caused an explosion of literacy.

4 & 5. **Telescope & microscope** - only by seeing things can we ask questions about their meaning.

Consider that most of the inventors of these five critical inventions and millions of others like them did not invent these things for money!

We should invent because that is our passion. We should become doctors, dentists, farmers, mechanics and whatever we desire because that is our passion. We will do whatever we choose to do, better providing opportunity for everyone to do what they love and everyone will benefit!

So during this transition, you will keep doing the jobs that you do for as long as needed to make the transition to the new paradigm.

We will use our incredible abilities to communicate to establish an orderly worldwide job posting and job fulfillment system.

If you are an auto mechanic and would rather be a farmer, you would post your job as an auto mechanic and look for a farmer who doesn't want to be a farmer. Without money being in the way, you could negotiate a swap of jobs and work out the details regarding transportation, location and living arrangements. Or, you could simply start working the job that you want right where you are.

If you are working at a fast food restaurant and you are working there because that is the only way that you could earn enough money to survive... You may consider doing something that you have always dreamed of. Now you can begin seeking the education that you previously could not afford so that you can pursue your dream.

What about the billions of people around the world who struggle to survive? Every day many simply have a mission to find food, water and shelter. What is in the way? Is there not enough food, water and shelter? NO! There is enough. We pay farmers in the United States NOT to farm! What is in the way is the monetary paradigm.

The plain, simple and UGLY truth is that there are plenty of resources but it is not PROFITABLE to help these people to survive and thrive.

In this transition, it is imperative that we focus on the logistics of ensuring these people are cared for first! If money is not in the way, we can instantly transport everything to the people in need everywhere!

In every factory around the world, we consider a new strategy. We now focus on how we build the best products possible utilizing all that technology can provide. We build products that are modular, reusable and will last. We automate every job possible so that people are freed up to have a great life experience!

Some may say that what I'm describing won't work because people will just stop working. People will just stay at home and play video games or go on permanent vacation. While that will be the case for some and especially in the beginning of the transition, there are many things to consider that will come into effect.

First of all, many people in the current monetary paradigm sit home playing video games and live off government welfare. Many others don't have to work because they were born into wealth or achieved wealth in some other way.

There will likely always be people who cannot contribute and people who are not motivated by anything to contribute. They are the exception, not the rule. Most of us just wish that we had more time to enjoy life. And, if we had more time to enjoy life, we wouldn't mind working so much.

If we build things that are made to last and things that are modular and reusable then we don't have to work as much to replace them. Our work weeks could go down to 1 or 2 days a week because we are not building things that get consumed just to keep feeding the monetary machine that is insatiable.

The other huge consideration to factor in is technology. Did you know that we are entering a phase of technological development that is and will continue to change the world in ways that are comparable to how the world was changed by the invention of the wheel?

With the recent advancements in nanotechnology, we will begin experiencing life in ways that have only been imagined in Science Fiction.

You may ask how this effects the "NEW GAME" paradigm shift and world peace.

For starters, lets consider the profound impact that absolutely FREE, clean energy will have on the world. That's right, "FREE" energy. The new clean energy based on nanotechnology where carbon 60 fibers are mixed in a solution and literally sprayed onto surfaces or impregnated into various surfaces allow entire buildings to become energy power plants.

So called "zero-point" energy could also be based on cold fusion or plasma. These emerging technologies by all accounts will render the old dirty energy useless!

What's more is that these new energies are clean and cannot be effectively metered by the money-hungry who currently leverage our need for energy to control us! This is a game changing development for the entire world!

Wars that are being fought for dirty energy resources will simply lose their steam as everyone gets free energy.

Disadvantaged countries will have electricity for their homes, businesses and for travel where they may not have been able to afford it in the past. This will effect manufacturing, farming and just about every aspect of development for human beings.

What if unrestricted travel were free? What if home heating and cooling were free?

This is not conjecture! This is going to happen before the end of this decade and most likely in the next 3 or 4 years.

The opportunity that this will create for world peace is immeasurable.

I have identified food, shelter, energy and water as cornerstones of freedom. Free energy will allow us to harvest water and food in addition to the obvious benefits of heat, cooling and energy for travel and production.

Nanotechnology will have a profound impact on our daily lives in other ways as well. For instance, we will manufacture materials at the molecular level. Self replicating machines have already been produced!

Regeneration of body-parts is also a reality. Did you know that if you were to cut the end of your finger off, you could apply what is affectionately called "Pixi Dust" to the injury and regrow the end of your finger including fingernail?

Technology is emphasizing that the monetary consumerism paradigm isn't working. Whats more is that technology is making monetary consumerism obsolete. This is a huge realization so let me repeat...

"technology is making monetary consumerism obsolete!"

The more that technology is applied, the less need we have for slave labor! The less need we have for people to act as if they were machines. Technology is critical to our freedom!

We must embrace and leverage every technological advantage available to us to make the transition.

If we all got this idea, believed in it and realized that together we can transform the world by shifting the paradigm, then we could do so with minimum suffering and chaos.

Transitioning will not be smooth or easy. It will take time and no doubt will require great courage and sacrifice.

FREEDOM is worth fighting for. We cannot begin to make a transition unless we all see the paradigm that we live in for what it is and see the solution in a new paradigm.

Once we all share the ideas and spread these ideas throughout the world, change and transition will soon follow.

Chapter 8 –Call To Action

This short book is not worth a second of time unless it results in action. Many of you will like the ideas presented and agree with the logic and philosophical reasoning.

And then, you are left with the same question you ask yourself when the guy shows up at your door with the pictures of starving children around the world. The question is: "What can I do?"

We all see our monetary, governing, political, social systems are broken and corrupt.

We all see the dire need for change but we feel helpless to do anything about it because the problems seem too big for us.

So, here is what you can do:

1. Spread the word. If you pass this information to your circle of friends and family through the various means available to you, then you have begun to make a difference. You have begun to become the change that you want to see in the world. Share this book freely! Give it away, copy it, post it on your own website.
2. Commit to being part of the paradigm shift and donate the money that you would spend on gifts, luxury and non-essential consumables to this

movement. Tell the people that you would have spent the money on what you are up to! We are in the "MONEY" paradigm and we will need to use money to shift the paradigm. Only the masses can provide the leverage in significant quantity to create the new game!

3. Believe and teach your children the concepts defined here and give them hope, desire and inspiration. Expand on these ideas and make them your own!

4. Become self-sufficient. Use the current technologies to get yourself off the grid with alternate energies. Make your home energy efficient. Plant a garden, raise some of your own livestock and stock up on seeds that will help you to survive in the worst conditions. The transition to this new paradigm will likely be rough and will take some time. Have enough water and food to survive. Now, is the time to take the first steps.

5. Vote out ALL of the incumbents in every government at every opportunity. Stop letting the few control us like we are animals. Take responsibility for yourself and for the future of humanity. Don't leave our future in the hands that have already proven time and time again that they only have their own best interests at heart.

6. Share your ideas and inventions openly and without concern for how much money you could

make if you patented them or manufactured them for profit. The money bubble will eventually burst and your contribution is needed now more than ever.

7. Keep working and producing locally no matter what happens. There are enough resources to provide all that we need.
This is critical!
What is likely to happen is that the current paradigm is going to collapse because it is not sustainable. When this happens, it will be up to all of us to work in cooperation not work in competition.
We will have to trust each other to stay at our posts and keep working to provide the essential services such as food, water, shelter and all the critical services such as police, fire, sanitary disposal, medical etc.
Keep producing right through the crisis as if nothing has changed because the only thing that can cause us to suffer is if we all believe that we must continue to play the monetary consumerism game. Before this happens, share this book and its concepts.

8. If you are in business it is especially important to share this with your suppliers and your employees. So, that when the time comes you can communicate with them and assure them that you are continuing to produce and so should

they! There will be many people who are not serving in a critical capacity. Bankers, people in sales, advertising and the manufacture of non-essential products. Billions of you will have the opportunity to volunteer your services to the critical sectors. This will seem uncomfortable to many but it is critical for everyone to contribute what they can to make the transition as smooth as possible.

We can do better and we will do better!

This has been a short read for most. It is my humble and sincere attempt to share my ideas and to create a grass root movement that all of humanity will consider.

The entire world is in a state of chaos and uncertainty. The paradigms that we have been living in amount to little more than slavery of humanity.

The predictable near future is scary if you listen to those who want to maintain control. For those of us who know that we can design a great life experience for humanity and live into our future, we can see this as an evolutionary opportunity for humanity!

I am of the opinion that in the next couple of years the monetary system will collapse and one of three things will likely happen.

1. We will sink into a global depression that will
    make the great depression of the past look like a
    walk in the park. Nobody wants this! More
    importantly, we can prevent it by simply not
    playing the old money game!

2. We will be presented with the new world order
    agenda and we will be told that we have to switch
    to a world currency in order to keep from going
    into a depression. This may sound like a
    tempting solution. It will be billed as a
    cooperative solution. Don't be fooled! This will
    only serve the wealthy minority that are served
    by monetary consumerism and will only extend
    our slavery!

3. We will all wake up and realize that the so called
    "financial crisis" is not real at all. It is just
    another twist in a game that we are playing.

    Think of it this way... When the money system
    collapses does that mean we just ran out of food,
    water or shelter? Does it mean that we just ran
    out of the raw materials to produce appliances,
    automobiles or tools? It doesn't mean any of
    those things!

    It only means that those who are controlling the
    masses through a corrupt monetary

consumerism paradigm are now changing the game and we are all supposed to follow along!

It is not real, and we don't have to play their game.

The opportunity is here for us to be FREE and play a new game! It is time for us to break free of this slavery and unite in a common and universal cause that is definitive and logical.

Those of us who have more than we need must let go of our self-centered fears. We must embrace the fact that if we help everyone to have what they need and ensure everyone's ability to thrive, then we are ensuring ourselves to have what we need and we will thrive!

This quote seems appropriate for those of you who do not believe in creating a new game that is based on a fundamental shift of the paradigm for which we live:

"You can't convince a believer of anything; for their belief is not based on evidence, it is based on deep seated need to believe." - Carl Sagan

Now, you have some idea of the issues and the potential solutions. Are you going to just sit on your butt, go back to work and live life as usual or are you going to make a positive difference in the world?

If you believe in God or if you believe in a higher intelligence in the universe or both, you have to ask yourself what would they think of the way we are living life on Earth.

Are you happy with the way that life on Earth is? Do you think that we are doing the best that we can as human beings or, do you think that we can do better?

I challenge you to world peace!

Anyone who has experienced "The Matrix" movie will appreciate that we are all now presented with a choice.

This book is your wake-up call telling you that it is a fact that we are all living in a game that was made up! You now can wake up from this game and choose to take the blue pill or the red pill.

Free yourself, your children and the generations of children to follow.... Take the "RED" pill – see how deep the rabbit hole goes!

The End...The Beginning

How much more corruption, violence and destruction must we all endure before we realize that we are on the wrong course?

Remember the 3 laws of humanity:

1. **Humans must ensure that others survive and thrive**
2. **Humans must themselves seek to survive and thrive without violating the first law**
3. **Humans must seek purpose without violating the first or second laws**

Please get involved and visit:
http://thenewgame.org

Also: search for "the new game" on Facebook

This is where you can actively participate or just stay in touch with what is happening. We need your genius!

As odd as it sounds... Donate if you can. We are still in the old game and every penny will be used for the cause. If you can't or you choose not to donate, at very least, freely pass this book on to everyone that you know and be part of the conscious evolution of humanity!

Let's all insist on designing a great life experience for EVERYONE!

www.ingramcontent.com/pod-product-compliance
Lightning Source LLC
Chambersburg PA
CBHW072332290526
45794CB00002B/844